PLANTS

AND

GOATS

AN EASY TO READ GUIDE

Felicity McCullough

Paperback Edition

ISBN-13: 978-1-78165-039-4

Plants And Goats An Easy To Read Guide

Copyright 2012 ©

My Lap Shop Publishers

Plymouth, England

www.mylapshop.com

www.goatlapshop.com

Series: **Goat Knowledge 6**

without a similar condition, including this condition, being imposed on the subsequent publisher. First Edition September 2012

Table of Contents

Disclaimer

This book is meant to be STRICTLY AN EDUCATIONAL AND INFORMATIONAL TOOL ONLY. The suggestions contained in this material might not be suitable for everyone. It is not intended to provide diagnosis or treatment. The author obtained the information from sources believed to be reliable and from personal experience. Although the best effort was made by the author, there are no guarantees as to the accuracy or completeness of the contents within this work.

The author does not guarantee the accuracy of any information or content in resources or websites listed or cited within this work. Additionally, the author, publisher and distributors never give medical, legal, accounting or any other type of professional advice. The reader must always seek those services from competent professionals that can review the particular circumstances. Mention of any product, brand or website is NOT an endorsement or recommendation of that product, service or usage.

The medical field is a very dynamic field that is constantly undergoing research, modifications and advancements and therefore information contained in this book should always be researched further and A VETERINARIAN OR OTHER SPECIALIST SHOULD BE CONSULTED where appropriate.

Any and all application of the information contained in this book is of the sole responsibility of the person performing said action. The author, publisher and distributors particularly disclaim any liability, loss, or risk taken by individuals who directly or indirectly act on the information herein. All readers must accept full responsibility for their use of this material.

Acknowledgements

The publisher thanks Danielle Shurskis for her support and help in bringing these series of books and articles to publication.

Introduction

Goats are ruminants, meaning that they have four "stomachs". These compartments are called the reticulum, rumen, omasum and abomasum. The abomasum is the compartment that corresponds to the "real stomach", which all animals have. The rumen is arguably the most important part of the gastrointestinal system. It is full of microorganisms which make it possible for the ruminant to eat hard, toughened plants that monogastrics, meaning one stomach, like us or other animals, can't digest.

Plants suffer rumination. A plant is eaten and mixed with saliva in the mouth. This goes through the oesophagus and enters the reticulum and then to the rumen. The rumen suffers a series of contractions which mixes up the plant particles with the rumen juices containing the microorganisms, which attack the plant particles, digesting them.

The plant particles need to be very small before they can continue their journey. If they are too big, they will cycle in the rumen and then will be regurgitated into the mouth where the ruminant will re-chew it, breaking it into smaller pieces. It is then returned to the reticulum.

After a time, the plant particles move on to the omasum and finally the abomasum, small intestines, large intestines and out of the body. Each section of the digestive system plays a part in digestion and absorption of nutrients.

Goats on Pasture

Goats can be kept on pasture. This is normal in meat goat operations. Even dairy goats can be kept on pasture, as long as they are supplemented with grain as needed. This is a technique often used to bring down the cost of feed and the labour involved … for part of the year at least, during the summer when the plants have their highest nutritional value.

Pasture Preparation

Whether or not you are preparing a pasture for the first time or revitalizing an older pasture, you will need to provide irrigation, fertilization, weed control and grazing management for your pastures in order to provide the best and most nutritious forages for your animals.

Before planting, you will need to prepare the seed bed. It may be necessary to apply a broad spectrum herbicide before tilling. Next, select which species you are going to plant. Below is a list of different species to be considered.

Usually pastures are planted from March through May and August through September. Seeds are planted normally at fifteen to twenty pounds per acre at a usual depth of ¼ inches. Planting is normally done by spreading the seed and then lightly dragging the field.

The most important aspect to creating a new pasture is PATIENCE. You will need to wait at least one season before letting your animals graze. Two seasons are necessary for pastures without irrigation. Allowing one cutting of hay will ensure that the plants are well established that they can't be simply uprooted by animals.

The plants in your pasture can be used as forage. It is the simplest way to utilize pasture. The plants can also be processed into hay or silage and stored for the winter.

Grasses

The following is a list of grasses by common name. This is a simple list for you to begin your research in grasses for pasture. Some are warm season, some are cold season. Some are annual and others perennial.

Some plants are high quality forage for animals, others are medium and yet others are low quality and are used for other reasons, like soil restoration or in cases where the soil is inappropriate for better plants.

When planning what to plant, we advise getting help from experts in your area in order to choose what species to plant. Each plant should be researched because many have cautions attached.

Annual Meadow-Grass

Antarctic Hair-Grass

Bluegrass

Cinnamon Grass

Cocksfoot or Orchardgrass

Common Bent

Couch-Grass

Creeping Bent

Creeping Red Fescue

Early Hair-Grass/Goose Grass

Land Tussac

Magellanic Bent

Magellanic Fescue

Marram Grass

Meadow Bromegrass

Meadow Fescue

Meadow Foxtail

Mountain Blue-Grass

Native Fog

Perennial Rye-Grass

Red Fescue

Reed Canary Grass

Shore Meadow-Grass

Silvery Hair-Grass

Smooth-Stalked   Meadow-Grass

Smooth Bromegrass

Sorghum

Squirrel-tail Fescue

Sudangrass

Sweet Vernal-Grass

Tall Fescue

Timothy Grass

Tussac

Wavy Hair-Grass

Whitegrass

Yorkshire Fog

Millet Grasses include:

Japanese

Proso

Foxtail

Barnyard

Koda

Finger

Plants And Goats An Easy To Read Guide

Teff

Pearl Millet

Forage Legumes

Legumes are often added to pasture for their high protein content and because they add organic nitrogen. They are normally added at one to two *pounds of seed per acre.*

Alfalfa

Alsike Clover

Birdsfoot Trefoil

Kura Clover

Marsh Birdsfoot Trefoil

Red Clover

Strawberry Clover

Sweet Clover

White Clover

Cereals

There are winter and spring cereals. At times pea plants are mixed in as well for added nutrition.

Barley

Fall Rye

Oat

Triticale

Winter Triticale

Winter Wheat

Other Plants

Brown Rush

Chicory

Christmas Bush

Corn

Diddle-Dee

Fachine

Mountain Berry

Native Rush

Native Woodrush

Plantain

Soybean

Tall Rush

Poisonous Plants

Although the rumen does provide some protection from poisonous plants, goats can easily suffer, or even die from ingesting poisonous plants.

The biggest problem with poisonous plants arises when the animals face starvation. In other words, when pasture is at its worst and the goat is forced to eat whatever it can, including poisonous plants. Another example of dangerous time for poisonings is in the early spring, because poisonous plants tend to be among the first to begin growing and those succulent green leaves look so good to the goat.

Plant poisoning can be accidental as well. A number of ornamental plants are actually poisonous. Do not feed garden clippings to goats.

Plant poisoning can vary in severity from no visible effects to sudden death depending on a number of factors, including how much of the plant was eaten and which part of the plant was eaten. The plants listed here are only a portion of plants that can be poisonous to goats. Check with people in your area for a list of poisonous plants in your area.

There are a number of substances within plants that can poison animals. These substances are important to know when treating animals that have been poisoned. Plants can contain more than one substance. Sometimes even plants that are normally safe to eat can become poisonous.

These substances are often contained in a specific part of the plant, for instance in wilted leaves or in roots or in the fruit. Plant poisoning depends on eating that specific part, which may not be available at all times. Another consideration is how much of the plant the goat eats. Normally, the goat needs to eat a lot.

Cyanogenic Plants

The poisonous substances in these plants are prussic acid or Hydrocyanic acid, a glycoside which interferes with oxygen in the blood. Sudden death is common with these plants as well as muscle tremors, rapid breathing and convulsions. Cyanogenic plants include:

Arrow Grass

Black Locust

Black Nightshade

Blue Cohosh Broomcarn

Buckeye/Horse Chestnut

Choke Cherry

Common Milkweed.

Corn Cockle

Dogbane

Elderberry

Hemp

Horse Nettle

Indian Hemp

Johnson Grass

Kafir

Laurel Leucothoe

Lily-Of-The-Valley

Maleberry

Marsh-Arrow Grass

Marijuana

Milkweed

Milo

Mountain Laurel

Nightshade

Oleander

Other Stone Fruits

Peaches

Plums

Rhododendron

Sevenbark

Silver Sneezewood

Sorghums *can be poisonous when leaves wilt after a frost or storm*

Stagger Brush

Sudan Grass

Velvet Grass

Water Hemlock

White Snakeroot

Wild Black Cherry

Wild Cherry

Wild Hydrangea

Alkaloids

Most livestock won't eat these plants because they have a bitter taste and irritate the gastrointestinal tract, causing nausea, diarrhoea, colic, muscular weakness, convulsions, death and blindness.

Some Alkaloids are: -

Aconite

Allspice

Black Snake Root

Bloodroot

Blue Cohosh

Boxwood

Buttercups

Celandine

Common Poppy

Crotalaria

Crow Poison

Death Camas

Dicentra

Dutches Breeches

False Hellebore

False Jessamine

Fume Wort

Hellebore

Hemp

Horse Nettle

Indian Hemp

Indian Poke

Jimson Weed

Larkspur

Lobelia

Lupines

Marsh Marigolds

Marijuana

Mayapple,

Monkshood

Moonseed

Nightshade

Pink Death Camas

Poison Darnel

Poison Hemlock

Poison Rye Grass

Pokeweed

Rattleweed

Rock Poppy

Spider Lily

Spotted Cowbane

Spotted Water Hemlock

Squirrel Corn

Stagger Grass

Staggerweed

Sweet Shrub

Thorn Apple

Varebells

Water Hemlock

Wild Parsnip

Wolfs-Bane

Yellow Jessamine

Photodynamic Plants

Photodynamic plants cause a reaction in animals with white, unpigmented areas of skin when exposed to bright sunlight. White goats may even die from this condition, if enough of the plant is eaten.

Alsike Clover

Buckwheat

Goat Weed

Klamath Weed

Lantana

Ornamental Hypericums

Rape

St. John's Wort

Saponin Glycosides

Saponin Glycosides cause violent gastroenteritis, vomiting, diarrhoea and colic. In the blood stream, it will destroy red blood cells and attack the Central Nervous System, causing convulsions and even paralysis.

Purple Cockle
Bouncing Bet
Pokeweed

Nitrate Poisoning

Nitrate is transformed into nitrite in the goat's gut and then absorbed into the blood. Nitrite then transforms haemoglobin into methemoglobin, which is toxic. Symptoms of this type of poisoning include trembling, staggering, rapid breathing and death as well as poor milk production and abortions in chronic cases. Nitrates can accumulate in the following plants:

Barley

Broccoli

Celery

Corn

Cucumbers

Kale

Milk Thistle

Oats

Poison Hemlock

Prickly Lettuce

Prostrate Pigweed

Rape

Rough Pigweed

Rutabaga

Rye

Sorghum,

Sow Thistle

Squash

Sudan Grass

Sugar Beets

Tumbling

Turnips

Wheat

Other Poisonous Plants

Bagpod

Baneberry

Black Oak

Bracken Fern

Buttercups

Coffee Weed

Crowfoot

Delphinium

Discarded Christmas Trees

Ground Ivy

Inkberry

Larkspur

Oak

Pin Cherry

Poison Ivy

Poke Weed

Ponderosa Pine Needles

Purple Sesban

Rattlebox

Snakeberry

Soapwort

Spurge

White Cohish.

Yew

Mechanical Injury

Certain plants can cause injury to the goat due to spines, beards, or fine hairs that gather in the goat's stomach to form balls.

Clover

Cocklebur

Downy Brome Grass

Mesquite

Poverty Grass

Sand Bur

Squirrel-Tail Grass

Renting Out Goats

Because goats are natural browsers, they are perfect for controlling invasive plants. You can set up a business with the primary goal of renting out your goats to clear brush and browse, or it can be more of a side or part-time business.

Using goats can be an inexpensive, easy and fast way to control invasive plants and clear land of brush than mechanically removing the plants or using chemical control with herbicides. It is also better for the environment if fewer chemicals are used.

Renting out goats can be your main operation and specifically why you are raising goats or a side enterprise for goat producers.

Preparation

If you are looking to rent out goats for controlling invasive plants, you will need to get involved. First, you will need to visit the site and evaluate the terrain, what will be needed in terms of fencing and guardian animals, if necessary and the plant species present.

Not every job is appropriate for goat foraging. Goats are best used when an area has been completely overrun by invasive plants. Goats will eat everything, including the bark of trees and beneficial plants. So, if there are a lot of beneficial plants that you don't want to be eaten and there are too many to be protected with temporary fencing, you may want to consider manual removal, or other means.

If you do decide to use goats, you will need to prepare the area for fencing. Fencing needs to be well-built because goats are excellent escape artists, making this a possible challenge. Fencing types that are most often used as temporary electric fencing include smooth wire, Polywire, tape, netting and rope.

You also need to consider predator control. Make sure you know what predators are in your area. Remember that even the neighbourhood dogs are predatory to goats. You may need to keep a guardian dog, donkey, or llama with the goats to keep the predators away. Sometimes simply using electric fencing works.

Management

You will also need to transport the goats to the site. This is normally done with a specific truck. Using a large herd on an area is advisable because of the competition factor. Goats are herd animals and have a hierarchy with dominant and submissive animals. They will compete with each other and eat more, faster.

You will need to visit your goats every day. They need to be checked on to make sure that they are okay and none are tangled in the fence or anything. Also, keep your eyes open for any sick animals and keep an eye on their hooves. If they are supplemented with grain, they will need to be fed every day and the water needs to be checked.

Goats, like all living things, need water, food, shade and shelter. The food isn't a problem, since that is what they are there for. The shade and shelter can be provided with temporary housing. Goats are notorious for hating water and will need protection from rain.

Choosing the Right Animal for the Job

Choosing which goats to use to keep invasive plants under control depends on a number of factors, including species, breed, sex, age, condition, health and even individual factors.

Preferred Species

Goats love invasive plants and browse that you want to get rid of. Some examples of these types of plants are: Poison Ivy, Bittersweet, Multiflora Rose, Japanese Stilt Grass, Greenbriar, Kudzu, Mile-A-

Minute, and Wine Berry. Some examples of plants that are beneficial and you will probably want to keep are Sweet Gum, Poplar, Maple, Oak, and Red Ceder.

Goats will eat all the leaves and small stems up to six or seven feet high. They target flower heads and seeds. There will get a bit of re-sprouting, meaning that repeated grazing is necessary. In the end, the goats will improve access and visibility of the site and can even wipe out the invasive plants if properly managed.

Species

Goats are browser and selective grazers that will eat the plants from the top down. They tolerate secondary compounds very well and are very agile to get their food, reaching high forage. In fact, you will need to protect your trees well, because they can reach it easily and are very capable of destroying young trees.

Goats are agile animals, meaning that they can get plants that other animals can't. They can graze up to six or seven feet off the ground even. Their anatomy makes them perfect selective grazers. They will eat the best and most nutritious part of the plant first.

Goats are smaller than sheep and cows. Smaller animals need a more nutrition-condensed diet, which is why they are more selective than sheep and cows.

Breed

There are a number of goat breeds. In essence, there is little difference between goat breeds. Grazing preference, management needs, disease and environmental stress tolerances are a few differences, for instance. In fact, when considering goat breeds, there are probably more differences within a breed than between breeds.

Crossbreeding is a technique used when individuals from two breeds are crossed together. The resulting goats often tend to be hardier because they get the best of both breeds.

Sex

The sex of the animal usually interferes with how easy they are to handle. Females and wethers, or castrated males, are easier to handle than intact males. Males tend to have an offensive odour during mating season because they spray their beards and legs with urine, which might create negative public perception. Intact males and females need to be kept apart.

Age

Older animals are easiest to handle and to move around. Kids need to stay with their mothers to learn how to eat. Kids are more likely to try novelty foods, have higher nutritional requirements and are less tolerant of environmental stresses and disease challenges. So, kids may not be the best for this job especially because they require better quality feed.

Condition

The term Condition here refers to the goat's state, including whether or not it is horned, their status in life and if they are healthy.

Most goats naturally have horns. Goats without horns are disbudded, or polled. Polled goats are born without horns. Horned animals can be more difficult to handle and they tend to get entangled in fences and feeders more easily. They need more space in practically everything as well, such as feeders and waterers. Horned animals should not be mixed with animals that don't have horns, wether disbudded or polled.

Consider the goat's status in life. Are they kids and are still growing? Then they will require a feed with a high quality and quantity of nutrition. Are they gestating? If they are in early to mid-gestation, perhaps you can use them, because their nutritional requirements are still low. Goats in late gestation and lactation, especially early lactation though have the highest needs. Goats near the end of their lactation may have low enough nutritional needs that they can be used. Goats that are only in maintenance are the best to use, because the browse is usually enough to fill their nutritional needs.

The goat's health is also an important factor. Look at its general appearance including hair coat, body condition and thriftiness. A thrifty animal simply looks and acts healthy. Is there evidence of disease, of external or internal parasites? What about its hooves, are they healthy? Check the herd records to make sure that vaccinations for Clostridial diseases and Rabies are up to date. Vaccinating for Rabies is a good idea because these goats are being exposed to the public.

Purchasing Animals

Look for local breeders and purchase animals. There are companies that offer fee-based grazing services. Visit the local county extension office, or equivalent for recommendations. Search online, including online directories. Look for listings in farm publications. You can look

for public livestock auctions, or
free give-away, or rescue
animals.

Resources

McAdam, Jim and Rodgrigo Olave. Falkland Islands: Pasture Plant Guide. Department of Agriculture. Available at: - http://www.afbini.gov.uk/falkland-islands-pasture-plant-guide.pdf.

McKenzie-Jakes, Angela. Getting Started in the Meat Goat Business: Plants Poisonous to Goats and Other Livestock in the Southeast. Florida A&M University.

Ministry of Agriculture, Food and Rural Affairs. Forages: Species.

Available at
http://www.omafra.gov.on.ca/eng
lish/crops/pub811/3species.htm#
grasses

National Agricultural Library.
Poisonous Plants. Extention
Goat Handbook. Available at
http://netvet.wustl.edu/species/go
ats/goatpois.txt

Schoenian, Susan, Brian Knox,
and Nevin Dawson. Goats and
Sheep: A Weapon Against
Weeds. July 22, 2010.

Utah State University. Pastures.
Available at: -

http://extension.usu.edu/smac/ht m/pastures/.

Published By:

My Lap Shop Publishers

91 Mayflower Street, Unit 222,

Plymouth, Devon, PL1 1SB

United Kingdom

Tel: +44 (0)871 560 5297

www.mylapshop.com

www.goatlapshop.com

About My Lap Shop Publishers

http://www.mylapshop.com/about

.htm

First Edition September 2012

ISBN - 978-1-78165-039-4

About Felicity McCullough

Felicity McCullough has written several books about preventative health care for goats. The website dedicated to goats www.goatlapshop.com has a wide variety of topics and resources that relate to goats, including the Charlie And Isabella's Magical Adventures Series of Children's Books, suitable for bed-time reading that are beautifully illustrated.

Goat Knowledge Series Titles:

How To Keep Goats Healthy #1

Golden Guernsey Goats #2

A Simple Guide To The Goat's Digestive System #3

Success Guide For Raising Healthy Goats #4

Managing Goat Nutrition: What You Need To Know A Simple Guide #5

Other Goat Books And Articles
By Felicity McCullough

www.goatlapshop.com

Boar Goats

Charlie And Isabella's Magical

Adventure

Charlie And Isabella Meet Jacob

Charlie And Isabella's Second

Adventure With Jacob

Charlie And Isabella's Magical

Adventures Compendium

Diseases of Goats

Goat Basics

Goat Breed: Golden Guernsey

Goats

Goat Videos

How To Keep Goats Healthy

Nigerian Dwarf Goats

Nimbkar Boer Goat

Raising Goats Easy Guide To

Raising and Caring for Goats

The Fun of Goats

My Lap Shop Publishers

Plymouth, England

www.mylapshop.com

www.goatlapshop.com

www.ingramcontent.com/pod-product-compliance
Lightning Source LLC
Chambersburg PA
CBHW070931270326
41927CB00011B/2811